I0012245

30-Day .NET Challenge: Recap of

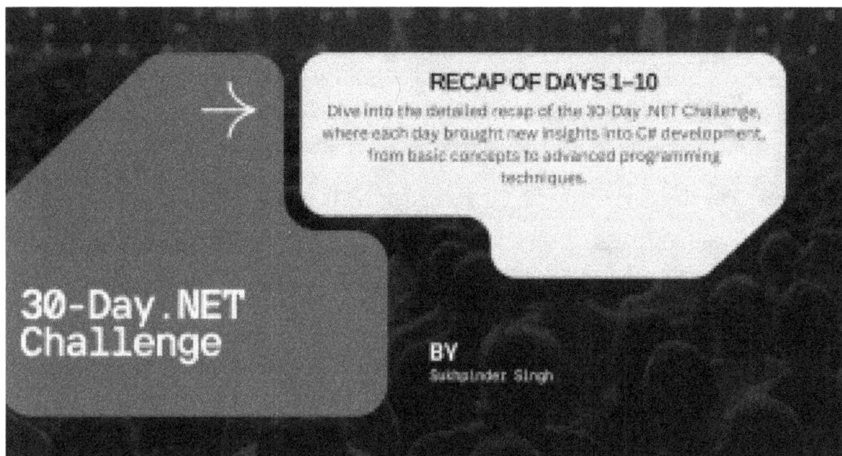
RECAP OF DAYS 1–10
Dive into the detailed recap of the 30-Day .NET Challenge, where each day brought new insights into C# development, from basic concepts to advanced programming techniques.
30-Day.NET Challenge
BY
Sukhpinder Singh

Day 1 of 30-Day .NET Challenge: Boolean Expressions

Introduction

The article discusses the foundational aspects of decision logic in C# programming. It focuses on Boolean expressions and operators and their importance for developers working on C# applications that deal with customer data and user inputs.

Learning Objectives:

1. Use operators to construct Boolean expressions for comparison and equality testing.
2. Employ built-in string class methods for efficient string evaluations.

Prerequisites for Developers

- Prior experience with basic coding tasks like variable instantiation, data type usage, and console output handling.
- Familiarity with `if-else` constructs for conditional statements.
- Understanding of using the Random class for generating random numbers.
- Proficiency in using **Visual Studio** or **Visual Studio Code** for creating and executing simple console applications.

Getting Started

What is an Expression?

An expression in programming combines values, operators, and methods to produce a single result. In C#, expressions are used within statements, such as "if" statements, to make decisions based on `true` or `false` outcomes. Boolean expressions, which return `true` or `false`, are pivotal for directing code execution and determining which code blocks to run. Developers select operators like equality (`==`) within Boolean expressions to compare values and guide program flow based on specific conditions and logic.

Equality Operator

To begin, create a static class file called "`Expressions.cs`" within the console application. Insert the provided code snippet into this file.

```
public static class Expressions
{
    /// <summary>
    /// Outputs
    /// True
    /// False
    /// False
    /// True
    /// </summary>
    public static void CheckEqualityOperator()
    {
        Console.WriteLine("a" == "a");
        Console.WriteLine("a" == "A");
        Console.WriteLine(1 == 2);
        string myValue = "a";
        Console.WriteLine(myValue == "a");
    }
}
```

Execute the code from the main method as follows

```
#region Day 1 - Expressions
using _30DayChallenge.Net.Day1;
Expressions.CheckEqualityOperator();
#endregion
```

Console Output

```
// Console Output
True
False
False
True
```

Enhance the comparison

We can improve the comparison for string equality by utilizing the string's inherent helper functionalities. It may seem unexpected that the line `Console.WriteLine("a" == "A");` returns false. Remember, string comparisons are case-sensitive.

Let's explore another scenario:

```
Console.WriteLine("a" == "a ");
```

In this example, a space is added at the end of one string. Consequently, this expression also yields false.

Enhance the previous equality check by applying these helper methods to both values, as demonstrated in the following code snippet:

```
/// <summary>
/// Outputs
/// True
/// </summary>
public static void CheckEqualityBuiltInMethods() {
    string value1 = " a";
    string value2 = "A ";
    Console.WriteLine(value1.Trim().ToLower() == value2.Trim().ToLower());
}
```

Execute the code from the main method as follows

```
#region Day 1 - Expressions
using _30DayChallenge.Net.Day1;
Expressions.CheckEqualityBuiltInMethods();
#endregion
```

Console Output

```
// Console Output
True
```

Inequality Operator

The inequality operator's result is the reverse of what the equality operator yielded.

Add another function to the `Expressions.cs` class as follows

```
/// <summary>
/// Outputs
/// False
/// True
/// True
/// False
/// </summary>
public static void CheckInEqualityOperator()
{
    Console.WriteLine("a" != "a");
    Console.WriteLine("a" != "A");
    Console.WriteLine(1 != 2);
    string myValue = "a";
    Console.WriteLine(myValue != "a");
}
```

Execute the code from the main method as follows

```
#region Day 1 - Expressions
using _30DayChallenge.Net.Day1;
Expressions.CheckInEqualityOperator();
#endregion
```

Console Output

```
// Console Output
False
True
True
False
```

Evaluating comparisons

For numeric comparisons, utilize operators such as:

- Greater than (>)
- Less than (<)
- Greater than or equal to (>=)
- Less than or equal to (<=)

Add another function to the `Expressions.cs` class as follows

```
/// <summary>
/// Outputs
/// False
/// True
/// True
/// True
/// </summary>
public static void CheckComparisonOperator()
{
    Console.WriteLine(1 > 2);
    Console.WriteLine(1 < 2);
    Console.WriteLine(1 >= 1);
    Console.WriteLine(1 <= 1);
}
```

Execute the code from the main method as follows

```
#region Day 1 - Expressions
using _30DayChallenge.Net.Day1;
Expressions.CheckComparisonOperator();
#endregion
```

Console Output

```
// Console Output
False
True
True
True
```

Boolean return type

Certain methods in programming return a Boolean value (`true` or `false`). In this exercise, utilize a built-in method from the `String` class to check if a larger string contains a specific word or phrase.

Add another function to the `Expressions.cs` class as follows

```
/// <summary>
/// Check if method contains a substring
/// </summary>
public static void CheckBooleanMethods()
{
    string pangram = "The quick brown fox jumps over the lazy dog.";
    Console.WriteLine(pangram.Contains("fox"));
    Console.WriteLine(pangram.Contains("cow"));
}
```

Execute the code from the main method as follows

```
#region Day 1 - Expressions
using _30DayChallenge.Net.Day1;
Expressions.CheckBooleanMethods();
#endregion
```

Console Output

```
// Console Output
True
False
```

Day 2 of 30-Day .NET Challenge: Variable Scope & Logic Control with Code Blocks

Introduction

Code blocks in programming are essential for grouping code lines and controlling variable accessibility. Variable scope, which determines where a variable can be accessed, is influenced by code blocks.

Learning Objectives:

Gain insight into the implications of declaring and initializing variables within and outside code blocks.

Prerequisites for Developers

- Declaring and initializing variables.
- Utilizing `if-else` selection statements.
- Employing `foreach` iteration statements.
- Calling methods from classes within the .NET Class Library.

Getting Started

How do code blocks impact variable scope?

Code blocks play a crucial role in determining the scope of variable declarations. Variable scope refers to the visibility of a variable within your application's code. A variable declared within a code block is locally scoped, meaning it is accessible only within that specific block. Attempting to access the variable outside the block will result in a compiler error.

Declare a variable inside the code block

To begin, create a static class file called "`CodeBlocksAndScope.cs`" within the console application. Insert the provided code snippet into this file.

```
/// <summary>
/// Output
/// Inside the code block: 10
/// </summary>
public static void VariableInCodeBlock()
{
    bool flag = true;
    if (flag)
    {
        int value = 10;
        Console.WriteLine($"Inside the code block: {value}");
    }
}
```

Execute the code from the main method as follows

```
#region Day 2 - Variable Scope & Logic Control with Code Blocks
CodeBlocksAndScope.VariableInCodeBlock();
#endregion
```

Console Output

```
// Console Output
Inside the code block: 10
```

Access a variable outside the code block

Add another method into the same static class wherein the code attempts to access the variable outside the code block

```
/// <summary>
/// Outputs
/// Program.cs(7,46): error CS0103: The name 'value' does not exist in the current
context
/// </summary>
public static void VariableOutCodeBlock()
{
    bool flag = true;
    if (flag)
    {
        int value = 10;
        Console.WriteLine($"Inside the code block: {value}");
    }
    //Uncomment below line to validate
    //Console.WriteLine($"Outside the code block: {value}");
}
```

Execute the code from the main method as follows

```
#region Day 2 - Variable Scope & Logic Control with Code Blocks
CodeBlocksAndScope.VariableOutCodeBlock();
#endregion
```

Console Output

```
// Console Output
Progran.cs(7,46): error CS0103: The name 'value' does not exist in the current
context
```

This error is generated because a variable that's declared inside a code block is only accessible within that code block.

Declare a variable unassigned above the code block & access inside the block

Add another method into the same static class wherein the code attempts to access the variable i.e. declared above the code block but it is not initialized.

```
/// <summary>
/// Outputs
/// Progran.cs(6,49): error CS0165: Use of unassigned local variable 'value'
/// </summary>
public static void VariableAboveCodeBlock()
{
    bool flag = true;
    int value;
    if (flag)
    {
        //Uncomment below line to validate
        //Console.WriteLine($"Inside the code block: {value}");
    }
    value = 10;
    Console.WriteLine($"Outside the code block: {value}");
}
```

Execute the code from the main method as follows

```
#region Day 2 - Variable Scope & Logic Control with Code Blocks
CodeBlocksAndScope.VariableAboveCodeBlock();
#endregion
```

Console Output

```
// Console Output
Progran.cs(6,49): error CS0165: Use of unassigned local variable 'value'
```

Declare a variable assigned above the code block & access inside the block

Add another method into the same static class wherein the code attempts to access the variable i.e. declared above the code block and assign a value

```
/// <summary>
/// Outputs
/// Inside the code block: 0
/// Outside the code block: 10
/// </summary>
/// <returns></returns>
public static void VariableAboveCodeBlockv1()
{
    bool flag = true;
    int value = 0;
    if (flag)
    {
        Console.WriteLine($"Inside the code block: {value}");
    }
    value = 10;
    Console.WriteLine($"Outside the code block: {value}");
}
```

Execute the code from the main method as follows

```
#region Day 2 - Variable Scope & Logic Control with Code Blocks
CodeBlocksAndScope.VariableAboveCodeBlockv1();
#endregion
```

Console Output

```
// Console Output
Inside the code block: 0
Outside the code block: 10
```

Day 3 of 30-Day .NET Challenge: Switch Constructs

Introduction

The switch statements are available for creating branching logic, each offering distinct advantages based on readability and maintenance.

Learning Objectives

Utilize the switch-case construct to compare a variable or expression with multiple potential outcomes.

Prerequisites for Developers

- Utilizing the `if-else` construct to incorporate branching logic.
- Handling variables, employing string interpolation, and displaying output.

Getting Started

What is a switch statement?

The switch statement selects and executes a specific section of code from a list of options known as switch sections. This selection is made by matching the switch expression with predefined patterns in the switch sections.

Basic Example

```
switch (fruit)
{
    case "apple":
        Console.WriteLine($"App will display information for apple.");
        break;
    case "banana":
        Console.WriteLine($"App will display information for banana.");
        break;
    case "cherry":
        Console.WriteLine($"App will display information for cherry.");
        break;
}
```

Basic Switch Example

To begin, create a static class file called "`Switch.cs`" within the console application. Insert the provided code snippet into this file.

```
static int employeeLevel = 200;
static string employeeName = "John Smith";

/// <summary>
/// Outputs
/// John Smith, Senior Associate
/// </summary>
public static void SwitchExample()
{
    string title = "";
    switch (employeeLevel)
    {
        case 100:
            title = "Junior Associate";
            break;
        case 200:
            title = "Senior Associate";
            break;
        case 300:
            title = "Manager";
            break;
        case 400:
            title = "Senior Manager";
            break;
        default:
            title = "Associate";
            break;
    }
    Console.WriteLine($"{employeeName}, {title}");
}
```

Execute the code from the main method as follows

```
#region Day 3 - Switch Constructs
Switch.SwitchExample();
#endregion
```

Console Output

```
// Console Output
John Smith, Senior Associate
```

Change Switch Label

Add another method into the same static class as shown below

```
static int employeeLevel = 200;
static string employeeName = "John Smith";

public static void SwitchExample()
{
    string title = "";
    switch (employeeLevel)
    {
        case 100:
            title = "Junior Associate";
            break;
        case 200:
            title = "Senior Associate";
            break;
        case 300:
            title = "Manager";
            break;
        case 400:
            title = "Senior Manager";
            break;
        default:
            title = "Associate";
            break;
    }
    Console.WriteLine($"{employeeName}, {title}");
}
/// <summary>
/// John Smith, Associate
/// </summary>
public static void ChangeSwitchLabelExample()
{
    employeeLevel = 201;
    SwitchExample();
}
```

Execute the code from the main method as follows

```
#region Day 3 - Switch Constructs
Switch.ChangeSwitchLabelExample();
#endregion
```

Console Output

```
// Console Output
John Smith, Associate
```

Multiple Switch Labels

Add another method into the same static class as shown below

```
/// <summary>
/// Outputs
/// John Smith, Senior Associate
/// </summary>
public static void MultipleSwitchLabelExample()
{
    int employeeLevel = 100;
    string employeeName = "John Smith";
    string title = "";
    switch (employeeLevel)
    {
        case 100:
        case 200:
            title = "Senior Associate";
            break;
        case 300:
            title = "Manager";
            break;
        case 400:
            title = "Senior Manager";
            break;
        default:
            title = "Associate";
            break;
    }
    Console.WriteLine($"{employeeName}, {title}");
}
```

Execute the code from the main method as follows

```
#region Day 3 - Switch Constructs
Switch.MultipleSwitchLabelExample();
#endregion
```

Console Output

```
// Console Output
John Smith, Senior Associate
```

Day 4 of 30-Day .NET Challenge: For Loops

Introduction

Welcome to this module `Day 4 of 30-Day .NET Challenge: For Loops`, where let's dive into the world of `for` statements. Explore how to write `for` statements that iterate a set number of times.

Learning Objectives

1. Utilize the `for` statement to iterate through a set of code.

Prerequisites for Developers

- Proficiency with the `foreach` iteration statement.
- Familiarity with working with variables.

Getting Started

What is the for statement?

The `for` statement allows you to iterate through a code block a fixed number of times, providing precise control over the iteration process.

Basic For Loop Example

To begin, create a static class file called "`ForLoop.cs`" within the console application. Insert the provided code snippet into this file.

```
/// <summary>
/// Outputs
/// 0
/// 1
/// 2
/// 3
/// 4
/// 5
/// 6
/// 7
/// 8
/// 9
/// </summary>
public static void ForLoopExample()
{
    for (int i = 0; i < 10; i++)
    {
        Console.WriteLine(i);
    }
}
```

Execute the code from the main method as follows

```
#region Day 4 - For Loops
ForLoops.ForLoopExample();
#endregion
```

13/79

Console Output

```
// Console Output
0
1
2
3
4
5
6
7
8
9
```

Run For Loop in reverse

The goal is to iterate through a code block while counting down instead of counting up.

Add another method into the same static class as shown below

```
/// <summary>
/// Outputs
/// 10
/// 9
/// 8
/// 7
/// 6
/// 5
/// 4
/// 3
/// 2
/// 1
/// 0
/// </summary>
public static void BackwardForLoopExample()
{
    for (int i = 10; i >= 0; i--)
    {
        Console.WriteLine(i);
    }
}
```

Execute the code from the main method as follows

```
#region Day 4 - For Loops
ForLoops.BackwardForLoopExample();
#endregion
```

Console Output

```
// Console Output
10
9
8
7
6
5
4
3
2
1
0
```

Iterative Pattern With For

The goal is to skip specific values in the iterator variable. Add another method into the same static class as shown below

```
/// <summary>
/// Outputs
/// 3
/// 6
/// 0
/// 9
/// </summary>
public static void IterationForLoopExample()
{
    for (int i = 0; i < 10; i += 3)
    {
        Console.WriteLine(i);
    }
}
```

Execute the code from the main method as follows

```
#region Day 4 - For Loops
ForLoops.IterationForLoopExample();
#endregion
```

Console Output

```
// Console Output
0
3
6
9
```

Break Loop

The goal is to exit the iteration statement prematurely based on some conditions. Add another method into the same static class as shown below

```
/// <summary>
/// Outputs
/// 0
/// 1
/// 2
/// 3
/// 4
/// 5
/// 6
/// 7
/// </summary>
public static void BreakForLoopExample()
{
    for (int i = 0; i < 10; i++)
    {
        Console.WriteLine(i);
        if (i == 7) break;
    }
}
```

Execute the code from the main method as follows

```
#region Day 4 - For Loops
ForLoops.BreakForLoopExample();
#endregion
```

Console Output

```
// Console Output
0
1
2
3
4
5
6
7
```

Day 5 of 30-Day .NET Challenge: While & do-while

Introduction

The do-while and while statements provide control over code execution flow by repeating a block of code until a condition is satisfied.

Learning Objectives

- Utilize the do-while loop to iterate through a code block.
- Implement the while loop to iterate through a code block as well.

Prerequisites for Developers

- Familiarity with utilizing the `if` statement.
- Proficiency in using `foreach` and `for` iteration statements.
- Competence in writing `Boolean` expressions.
- Knowledge of generating random numbers using the `System.Random` class and the `Random.Next()` method.

Getting Started

What is the do-while loop?

The do-while statement runs a statement or block of statements as long as a specified Boolean expression remains true. As this expression is evaluated after each loop execution, a do-while loop executes at least once.

Example: do-while

Let's create code that continuously generates random numbers ranging from 1 to 10 until we generate the number 7. The number 7 could be generated in one iteration or after several iterations.

To begin, create a static class file called "`WhileLoop.cs`" within the console application. Insert the provided code snippet into this file.

```
/// <summary>
/// Outputs
/// 2
/// 5
/// 8
/// 2
/// 7
/// </summary>
public static void DoWhileLoopExample()
{
    Random random = new Random();
    int current = 0;
    do
    {
        current = random.Next(1, 11);
        Console.WriteLine(current);
    } while (current != 7);
}
```

Execute the code from the main method as follows

```
#region Day 5 - While & do-while
WhileLoop.DoWhileLoopExample();
#endregion
```

Console Output

```
2
5
8
2
7
```

Example: while

The `while` statement will iterate based on the Boolean expression. To do that add another method into the same static class as shown below

```
/// <summary>
/// Outputs
/// 9
/// 7
/// 5
/// Last number: 1
/// </summary>
public static void WhileLoopExample()
{
    Random random = new Random();
    int current = random.Next(1, 11);
    while (current >= 3)
    {
        Console.WriteLine(current);
        current = random.Next(1, 11);
    }
    Console.WriteLine($"Last number: {current}");
}
```

Execute the code from the main method as follows

```
#region Day 5 - While & do-while
WhileLoop.WhileLoopExample();
#endregion
```

Console Output

```
9
7
5
Last number: 1
```

Continue statement with do-while

Sometimes, developers need to skip the rest of the code within a code block and move on to the next iteration. To achieve this add another method into the same static class as shown below

```
/// <summary>
/// Outputs
/// 5
/// 1
/// 6
/// 7
/// </summary>
public static void ContinueDoWhileLoopExample()
{
    Random random = new Random();
    int current = random.Next(1, 11);
    do
    {
        current = random.Next(1, 11);
        if (current >= 8) continue;
        Console.WriteLine(current);
    } while (current != 7);
}
```

Execute the code from the main method as follows

```
#region Day 5 - While & do-while
WhileLoop.ContinueDoWhileLoopExample();
#endregion
```

Console Output

```
5
1
6
7
```

Day 6 of 30-Day .NET Challenge: String built-in Methods

Introduction

The module demonstrates `string` helper methods to pinpoint and extract the desired information.

Learning Objectives

- Locate the position of a character or substring within another string
- Retrieve segments of strings

Prerequisites for Developers

- Basic familiarity with string helper methods
- Basic understanding of while iteration statements

- Proficiency in using Visual Studio or Visual Studio Code for C# code development, building, and execution

Getting Started

IndexOf method

Utilize the `IndexOf()` method to find the position of a single or multiple characters/strings within a larger string.

To begin, create a static class file called "`StringMethods.cs`" within the console application. Insert the provided code snippet into this file.

```
public static class StringMethods
{
    /// <summary>
    /// Outputs
    /// 13
    /// 36
    /// </summary>
    public static void IndexOfExample()
    {
        string message = "Find what is (inside the parentheses)";
        int openingPosition = message.IndexOf("(");
        int closingPosition = message.IndexOf(")");
        Console.WriteLine(openingPosition);
        Console.WriteLine(closingPosition);
    }
}
```

Execute the code from the main method as follows

```
#region Day 6 - String built-in methods
StringMethods.IndexOfExample();
#endregion
```

Console Output

```
13
36
```

Substring method

Use the Substring() method to extract the part of the main string that comes after the specified character positions.

To do that add another method into the same static class as shown below

```
/// <summary>
/// Outputs
/// (inside the parentheses
/// </summary>
public static void SubstringExample()
{
    string message = "Find what is (inside the parentheses)";
    int openingPosition = message.IndexOf('(');
    int closingPosition = message.IndexOf(')');
    int length = closingPosition - openingPosition;
    Console.WriteLine(message.Substring(openingPosition, length));
}
```

Execute the code from the main method as follows

```
#region Day 6 - String built-in methods
StringMethods.SubstringExample();
#endregion
```

Console Output

```
(inside the parentheses
```

Skip the first character "("

Simply update the starting index position using `openingPosition += 1;` To do that add another method into the same static class as shown below

```
/// <summary>
/// Outputs
/// inside the parentheses
/// </summary>
public static void SubstringExample2()
{
    string message = "Find what is (inside the parentheses)";
    int openingPosition = message.IndexOf('(');
    int closingPosition = message.IndexOf(')');
    openingPosition += 1;
    int length = closingPosition - openingPosition;
    Console.WriteLine(message.Substring(openingPosition, length));
}
```

Execute the code from the main method as follows

```
#region Day 6 - String built-in methods
StringMethods.SubstringExample2();
#endregion
```

Console Output

```
inside the parentheses
```

Day 7 of 30-Day .NET Challenge: String built-in Methods Part 2

Introduction

The article demonstrates the `IndexOfAny()` method to locate the initial occurrence of any string from a chosen array. Additionally, you utilize `LastIndexOf()` to pinpoint the last occurrence of a string within another string.

Learning Objectives

- Learn to use `LastIndexOf()` method
- Learn to use `IndexOfAny()` method

Prerequisites for Developers

- Basic familiarity with string helper methods
- Basic understanding of while iteration statements
- Proficiency in using Visual Studio or Visual Studio Code for C# code development, building, and execution

Getting Started

`LastIndexOf Method`

To enhance the complexity of the "`message`" variable by incorporating numerous sets of parentheses, followed by coding to extract the content enclosed within the last set of parentheses.

To begin, create a static class file called "`StringMethodsPart2.cs`" within the console application. Insert the provided code snippet into this file.

```
public static class StringMethodsPart2
{
    /// <summary>
    /// Outputs
    /// Searching THIS message: Help (find) the (opening symbols)
    /// Found WITHOUT using startPosition: (find) the ( opening symbols )
    /// </summary>
    public static void IndexOfAnyMethod()
    {
        string message = "Help (find) the (opening symbols)";
        Console.WriteLine($"Searching THIS Message: {message}");
        char[] openSymbols = ['[', '{', '('];
        int openingPosition = message.IndexOfAny(openSymbols);
        Console.WriteLine($"Found WITHOUT using startPosition:
{message.Substring(openingPosition)}");
    }
}
```

Execute the code from the main method as follows

```
#region Day 7 - String built-in methods Part 2
StringMethodsPart2.IndexOfAnyMethod();
#endregion
```

Console Output

```
set of parentheses
```

IndexOfAny Method

Utilize .IndexOfAny() to retrieve the index of the initial symbol from the openSymbols array that is present in the message string.

To do that add another method into the same static class as shown below

```
/// <summary>
/// Outputs
/// set of parentheses
/// </summary>
public static void LastIndexOfMethod() {

    string message = "(What if) I am (only interested) in the last (set of
parentheses)?";
    int openingPosition = message.LastIndexOf("(");

    openingPosition += 1;
    int closingPosition = message.LastIndexOf(")");
    int length = closingPosition - openingPosition;
    Console.WriteLine(message.Substring(openingPosition, length));
}
```

Execute the code from the main method as follows

```
#region Day 7 - String built-in methods Part 2
StringMethodsPart2.LastIndexOfMethod();
#endregion
```

Console Output

```
Searching THIS message: Help (find) the (opening symbols)
Found WITHOUT using startPosition: (find) the (opening symbols)
```

Day 8 of 30-Day .NET Challenge: Exception Handling

Introduction

Throughout this module, you will gain knowledge about exceptions, the process of handling exceptions, and the different exception-handing patterns that C# supports.

Learning Objectives:

- Examine the basic categories of exceptions and review some common system exceptions.

Prerequisites for Developers

- Visual Studio Code configured for C# application development
- Ability to create C# console applications with iteration, selection, and custom methods for business logic
- Understanding of error handling and exceptions in C#
- Experience using Visual Studio Code debugging tools for C#

Getting Started

In C#, exception handling is achieved through the utilization of the try, catch, and finally keywords. Each of these keywords is linked with a distinct code block and serves a particular purpose in managing exceptions.

To begin, create a static class file called "`ExceptionHandling.cs`" within the console application. Insert the provided code snippet into this file.

```
public static class ExceptionHandling
{
    /// <summary>
    /// Outputs
    /// Hello from try block
    /// Hello from exception block
    /// Hello from finally block
    /// </summary>
    public static void SimpleExceptionBlock()
    {
        try
        {
            // try code block - code that may generate an exception
            Console.WriteLine("Hello from try block");
            throw new NotImplementedException();
        }
        catch
        {
            // catch code block - code to handle an exception
            Console.WriteLine("Hello from exception block");
        }
        finally
        {
            // finally code block - code to clean up resources
            Console.WriteLine("Hello from finally block");
        }
    }
}
```

Execute the code from the main method as follows

```
#region Day 8 - Exception Handling
ExceptionHandling.SimpleExceptionBlock();
#endregion
```

Console Output

```
Hello from try block
Hello from exception block
Hello from finally block
```

Nested Exception Handling

Add another method into the same static class as shown below

```
/// <summary>
/// Outputs
/// Hello from try block
/// Hello from inner finally block
/// Hello from exception block
/// Hello from outer finally block
/// </summary>
public static void NestedExceptionBlock()
{
    try
    {
        // Step 1: code execution begins
        try
        {
            // Step 2: an exception occurs here
            Console.WriteLine("Hello from try block");
            throw new NotImplementedException();
        }
        finally
        {
            // Step 4: the system executes the finally code block associated with
the try statement where the exception occurred
            Console.WriteLine("Hello from inner finally block");
        }
    }
    catch // Step 3: the system finds a catch clause that can handle the exception
    {
        // Step 5: the system transfers control to the first line of the catch
code block
        Console.WriteLine("Hello from exception block");
    }
    finally
    {
        Console.WriteLine("Hello from outer finally block");
    }
}
```

In this scenario, the following sequence of events unfolds:

1. The program starts executing within the code block of the outer try statement.
2. An exception is triggered within the code block of the inner try statement.
3. The runtime identifies the catch clause linked to the outer try statement.

4. Before transferring control to the initial line of the catch code block, the runtime executes the final clause tied to the inner try statement.

5. Subsequently, control shifts to the beginning of the catch code block, where the code for handling the exception is executed.

Execute the code from the main method as follows

```
#region Day 8 - Exception Handling
ExceptionHandling.NestedExceptionBlock();
#endregion
```

Console Output

```
Hello from try block
Hello from inner finally block
Hello from exception block
Hello from outer finally block
```

Day 9 of 30-Day .NET Challenge: Null Safety

Introduction

The article demonstrates the use of null-state analysis to remove compiler warnings of "check code for null safety".

Learning Objectives

Discover how to set up the nullable context in your C# project or codebase.

Prerequisites for Developers

- Familiarity with introductory-level C# programming
- Know how to use Visual Studio Code or Visual Studio
- .NET SDK version 6.0 or newer

Getting Started

.NET developers often face the `System.NullReferenceException`, which happens when a null is referenced at runtime, which results in the most common exception in the .NET application

> As the creator of null, Sir Tony Hoare, refers to `null` as the "billion-dollar mistake."

Example

The variable `records` is set to null and then immediately referenced which results in `System.NullReferenceException`

```
TestRecord records = null;

_ = records.ToString();

record TestRecord(int Id, string Name);
```

As the applications grow in number of lines of code and become more complex, spotting such issues as a developer can be challenging.

> This is where C# compiler steps in.

Define null safety

In the previous example, a developer can avoid the `System.NullReferenceException`by checking if `records` variable was null as shown below

```
TestRecord records = null;

// Check for null
if (records is not null)
{
    _ = records.ToString();
}

record TestRecord(int Id, string Name);
```

Nullable Types

The `default` value for all reference types is `null`.

```
string first;                  // first is null
string second = string.Empty   // second is not null, instead it's an empty string
""
int third;                     // third is 0 because int is a value type
DateTime date;                 // date is DateTime.MinValue
```

In the example mentioned earlier:

- The variable "first" is null because a reference type "string" was declared but not assigned any value.
- The variable "second" is assigned the value "string.Empty" during declaration.
- The variable "third" has a value of 0 even though it was not explicitly assigned.
- The variable "date" is uninitialized, but its default value is "System.DateTime.MinValue."

Post C# 2.0 version, we can define nullable values using `Nullable<T>`. This allowed value types to be assigned with a value of null

```
int? first;            // first is implicitly null (uninitialized)
int? second = null;    // second is explicitly null
int? third = default;  // third is null as the default value for Nullable<Int32>
is null
int? fourth = new();    // fourth is 0, since new calls the nullable constructor
```

Nullable context

As per my experience, this is a must-have feature that should be enabled in every .Net application as it enables control for how the compiler understands reference type variables.

There are four types of nullable contexts

- disable
- enable
- warnings
- annotations

Enable nullable context

it can be enabled by adding `<Nullable>` item to the `<PropertyGroup>` inside the application `.csproj` file as shown below

```
<Project Sdk="Microsoft.NET.Sdk">

    <PropertyGroup>
        <OutputType>Exe</OutputType>
        <TargetFramework>net6.0</TargetFramework>
        <Nullable>enable</Nullable>
    </PropertyGroup>

    <!-- Omitted for brevity -->

</Project>
```

Alternatively, developers can also add scope nullable context which means the nullable context will be applicable only in the defined scope.

```
#nullable enable
```

Day 10 of 30-Day .NET Challenge: File Paths

Introduction

The article demonstrates the built-in functions while working with file system paths. It makes it easier to handle file paths.

Learning Objectives

Learn about constants and functions in the System.IO namespace

Prerequisites for Developers

- How to use Visual Studio or Visual Studio Code
- Handling variables, employing string interpolation, and displaying output.

Getting Started

How to determine the current directory?

The System.IO contains a method to expose the full path of the current directory. To begin, create a static class file called "FilePath.cs" within the console application. Insert the provided code snippet into this file.

```
public static class FilePath
{
    /// <summary>
    /// Outputs
    /// D:\Workspace\30DayChallenge.Net\30DayChallenge.Net\bin\Debug\net8.0
    /// </summary>
    public static void DisplayCurrentDirectory()
    {
        Console.WriteLine(Directory.GetCurrentDirectory());
    }
}
```

Execute the code from the main method as follows

```
#region Day 10 - File Path
FilePath.DisplayCurrentDirectory();
#endregion
```

Console Output

```
D:\Workspace\30DayChallenge.Net\30DayChallenge.Net\bin\Debug\net8.0
```

How to work with special directories?

The code below provides the path to the Windows My Documents folder equivalent or the user's HOME directory, regardless of the operating system, including Linux. To do that add another method into the same static class as shown below

```
/// <summary>
/// Outputs
/// C:\Users\admin\Documents
/// </summary>
public static void DisplaySpecialDirectory()
{

Console.WriteLine(Environment.GetFolderPath(Environment.SpecialFolder.MyDocuments)
);
}
```

Execute the code from the main method as follows

```
#region Day 10 - File Path
FilePath.DisplaySpecialDirectory();
#endregion
```

Console Output

```
C:\Users\admin\Documents
```

How to get OS path characters?

Various operating systems utilize distinct characters for separating directory levels. The framework automatically interprets the separator character relevant to the operating system being used.

To do that add another method into the same static class as shown below

```
/// <summary>
/// Outputs
/// For windows: \sample
/// </summary>
public static void DisplayOSPathCharacters()
{
    Console.WriteLine($"For windows: {Path.DirectorySeparatorChar}sample");
}
```

Execute the code from the main method as follows

```
#region Day 10 - File Path
FilePath.DisplayOSPathCharacters();
#endregion
```

Console Output

```
For windows: \sample
```

How do you get filename extensions?

The Path class also exposes a method to get an extension of any filename passed as a parameter. To do that add another method into the same static class as shown below

```
/// <summary>
/// Outputs
/// .json
/// </summary>
public static void DisplayFileExtension()
{
    Console.WriteLine(Path.GetExtension("sample.json"));
}
```

Execute the code from the main method as follows

```
#region Day 10 - File Path
FilePath.DisplayFileExtension();
#endregion
```

Console Output

```
.json
```

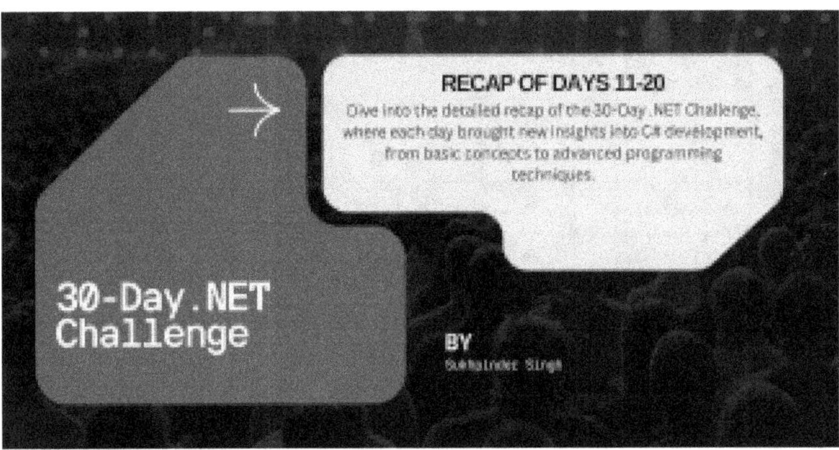
RECAP OF DAYS 11-20
Dive into the detailed recap of the 30-Day .NET Challenge, where each day brought new insights into C# development, from basic concepts to advanced programming techniques.
30-Day .NET Challenge
BY

Day 11 of 30-Day .NET Challenge: Helper Methods—Array

Introduction

The article demonstrates the use of various C# helper methods like Sort, Reverse, Clear and Resize.

Learning Objectives

- Learn how to use helper methods like `Sort()` and `Reverse()`
- Learn how to use helper methods like `Clear()` and `Resize()`

Prerequisites for Developers

- Familiar with `arrays`.
- Familiar with `if` statement
- Experience in running C# code through Visual Studio or Visual Studio Code.

Getting Started

How to use a Sort helper method

Utilize the Array class's `Sort()` method to arrange the elements in the array in alphanumeric order. To begin, create a static class file called "`ArrayHelperMethods.cs`" within the console application. Insert the provided code snippet into this file.

```
public static class ArrayHelperMethods
{
    /// <summary>
    /// Outputs
    /// Before Sorting...
    /// B14, A11, B12, A13
    /// After Sorting...
    /// A11, A13, B12, B14
    /// </summary>
    public static void SortExample()
    {
        Console.WriteLine("Before Sorting...");
        string[] pallets = { "B14", "A11", "B12", "A13" };
        Console.WriteLine(string.Join(",", pallets));
        Array.Sort(pallets);
        Console.WriteLine("After Sorting...");
        Console.WriteLine(string.Join(",", pallets));
    }
}
```

Execute the code from the main method as follows

```
#region Day 11 - Helper Methods  -  Array
ArrayHelperMethods.SortExample();
#endregion
```

Console Output

```
Before Sorting...
B14,A11,B12,A13
After Sorting...
A11,A13,B12,B14
```

How to use the Reverse helper method

In the following example, let's execute the `Reverse()` method from the Array class to invert the sequence of elements. To do that add another method into the same static class as shown below

```
/// <summary>
/// Outputs
/// Before Sorting...
/// B14,A11,B12,A13
/// After Reverse Sorting...
/// A13,B12,A11,B14
/// </summary>
public static void ReverseSortExample() {
Console.WriteLine("Before Sorting...");
    string[] pallets = { "B14", "A11", "B12", "A13" };
    Console.WriteLine(string.Join(",", pallets));
    Array.Reverse(pallets);
    Console.WriteLine("After Reverse Sorting...");
    Console.WriteLine(string.Join(",", pallets));
}
```

Execute the code from the main method as follows

```
#region Day 11 - Helper Methods  -  Array
ArrayHelperMethods.ReverseSortExample();
#endregion
```

Console Output

```
Before Sorting...
B14,A11,B12,A13
After Reverse Sorting...
A13,B12,A11,B14
```

How to use the Clear Helper method

The `Array.Clear()` method helps to clear the value of specified elements within the array. To do that add another method into the same static class as shown below

```
/// <summary>
/// Outputs
/// Clearing 2 ... count: 4
/// ,,B12,A13
/// </summary>
public static void ClearExample()
{
    string[] pallets = { "B14", "A11", "B12", "A13" };
    Console.WriteLine("");
Array.Clear(pallets, 0, 2);
    Console.WriteLine($"Clearing 2 ... count: {pallets.Length}");
    Console.WriteLine(string.Join(",", pallets));
}
```

Execute the code from the main method as follows

```
#region Day 11 - Helper Methods  -  Array
ArrayHelperMethods.ClearExample();
#endregion
```

Console Output

```
Clearing 2 ... count: 4
,,B12,A13
```

How to use the Resize helper method

In the following example, let's expand the array size from 4 to 6, then add two new numbers at index 4 and 5. The two newly added elements will remain null until the value is assigned.

```
/// <summary>
/// Outputs
/// B14,A11,B12,A13
/// Resizing 6 ... count: 6
/// B14,A11,B12,A13,C01,C02
/// </summary>
public static void ResizeAndAdd() {
    string[] pallets = { "B14", "A11", "B12", "A13" };
    Console.WriteLine(string.Join(",", pallets));
    Array.Resize(ref pallets, 6);
    Console.WriteLine($"Resizing 6 ... count: {pallets.Length}");
    pallets[4] = "C01";
    pallets[5] = "C02";
    Console.WriteLine(string.Join(",", pallets));
}
```

Execute the code from the main method as follows

```
#region Day 11 - Helper Methods - Array
ArrayHelperMethods.ResizeAndAdd();
#endregion
```

Console Output

```
B14,A11,B12,A13
Resizing 6 ... count: 6
B14,A11,B12,A13,C01,C02
```

Day 12 of 30-Day .NET Challenge: Azure Functions

Azure Functions are serverless applications on Microsoft Azure Cloud Platform without worrying about the infrastructure to run it. It's very similar to the lambda function in the AWS Cloud.

Introduction

Azure Functions are serverless applications on Microsoft Azure Cloud Platform without worrying about the infrastructure to run it. It's very similar to the lambda function in the AWS Cloud.

Learning Objectives

- Create a function using Visual Studio or Visual Studio Code

- Run an Azure function locally.

Prerequisites for Developers

- Experience with Visual Studio
- Basic understanding of C# Programming Language

Getting Started

Add a new function

1. Choose a project "Azure Function" from Visual Studio.
2. Select .Net 6 as the target version
3. Select the template "HTTP Trigger"
4. Provide a function name.
5. Choose Authorization Level as "Anonymous" which allows access to anyone to call your function endpoint.

Code

The below Azure Function returns a `string` message as follows

- If ?name= is passed then returns a message as `Hello, {name}. This HTTP triggered function executed successfully.`
- Else a general message is returned `This HTTP triggered function executed successfully. Pass a name in the query string or in the request body for a personalized response.`

```
public static class BasicExample
{
    [FunctionName("BasicExample")]
    public static async Task<IActionResult> Run(
        [HttpTrigger(AuthorizationLevel.Anonymous, "get", "post", Route = null)]
HttpRequest req,
        ILogger log)
    {
        log.LogInformation("C# HTTP trigger function processed a request.");
        string name = req.Query["name"];
        string requestBody = await new StreamReader(req.Body).ReadToEndAsync();
        dynamic data = JsonConvert.DeserializeObject(requestBody);
        name = name ?? data?.name;
        string responseMessage = string.IsNullOrEmpty(name)
            ? "This HTTP triggered function executed successfully. Pass a name in
the query string or in the request body for a personalized response."
            : $"Hello, {name}. This HTTP triggered function executed
successfully.";
        return new OkObjectResult(responseMessage);
    }
}
```

Test the function locally

Simply press F5 to start debugging the Azure function, it will open a console which will provide a URL to access the browser.

Console Output

```
Azure Functions Core Tools
Core Tools Version:       4.0.5198 Commit hash: N/A  (64-bit)
Function Runtime Version: 4.21.1.20667
[2024-03-28T05:48:45.707Z] Found
D:\Workspace\30DayChallenge.Net\AzureFunctionExample\AzureFunctionExample.csproj.
Using for user secrets file configuration.
Functions:
        BasicExample: [GET,POST] http://localhost:7073/api/BasicExample
```

Open the URL

Open the URL "http://localhost:7073/api/BasicExample" in the browser to start running the function endpoint.

The response returned from the browser.

```
This HTTP triggered function executed successfully. Pass a name in the query
string or in the request body for a personalized response.
```

Add query parameters

Modify the URL with additional query parameters as ?name=Sukhpinder

```
http://localhost:7073/api/BasicExample?name=Sukhpinder
```

The response returned from the browser.

```
Hello, Sukhpinder. This HTTP triggered function executed successfully.
```

Day 13 of the 30-Day .NET Challenge: `ConfigureAwait(false)`

The article demonstrates the use of `ConfigureAwait(false)` efficiently to add deadlock-free asynchronous code.

Introduction

The article demonstrates the use of `ConfigureAwait(false)` efficiently to add deadlock-free asynchronous code.

Learning Objectives

- How to use `ConfigureAwait(false)` instead of traditional async await programming
- Why `ConfigureAwait(false)` is better

Prerequisites for Developers

- Basic understanding of C# programming language
- Basic understanding of asynchronous programming using async await

Getting Started

Consider an example where the user wants to load data asynchronously within a method.

```
/// <summary>
/// Old approach with classic async await
/// </summary>
/// <returns></returns>
public async static Task OldApproach()
{
    await ReadDataAsync();
}
```

In this approach, the await operator waits for `ReadDataAsync` then proceeds with execution in the same synchronization context from where it began

The aforementioned approach is used when the developer ensures that UI updates are executed in a separate thread. However, it may introduce potential deadlock risks.

Optimized approach with `ConfigureAwait(false)`.

Let's transform the above method using `ConfigureAwait(false)`

```
/// <summary>
/// Optimized approach with ConfigureAwait
/// </summary>
/// <returns></returns>
public static async Task OptimizedApproachAsync()
{
    await ReadDataAsync().ConfigureAwait(false);
}
```

By adding this, the compiler doesn't add the execution in the same synchronization context which reduces the chances of deadlocks.

The aforementioned optimization is beneficial in non-UI applications like library code etc.

Why `ConfigureAwait(false)` is better

Please find below the benefits of using `ConfigureAwait(false)` method

Improved Performance

As the optimized approach doesn't add the execution to the same synchronization context, it saves on extra overhead and helps create scalable applications.

Reduce chances of deadlocks

`ConfigureAwait(false)` method mitigates the risk of deadlocks when the synchronization context is blocked.

Conclusion

The `ConfigureAwait(false)` method in C# aiming to craft efficient, deadlock-avoidant asynchronous code. Its advantages are particularly beneficial in non-UI applications and in library projects.

Complete Code on GitHub

GitHub — ssukhpinder/30DayChallenge.Net
*Contribute to ssukhpinder/30DayChallenge.Net development by creating an account on GitHub.*github.com

Day 14 of 30-Day .NET Challenge: Limit Concurrent Async Operations

The article highlights the importance of limiting the concurrent asynchronous operations which in turn improves performance.

Introduction

The article highlights the importance of limiting the concurrent asynchronous operations which in turn improves performance.

Learning Objectives

- The common mistake all developers do
- How to use limit concurrent async operations
- Best Practices

Prerequisites for Developers

- Basic understanding of C# programming language
- Basic understanding of asynchronous programming using async await

Getting Started

The common mistake all developers do

Consider an example where the user wants to load data asynchronously within a method and it highlights the common mistake developers make

```
(async item => await ProcessItem(item));

/// <summary>
/// Old approach with classic async await
/// </summary>
/// <returns></returns>
public async static Task OldApproach(List<string> items)
{
    var tasks = items.Select(async item => await ProcessItem(item));
    await Task.WhenAll(tasks);
}
```

The approach may look clean and simple but it initiates tasks for each item in the collection concurrently. This can cause system strain under heavy `List<string> items` which will produce poor application performance.

Optimized approach with `Concurrency Limit`

Let's transform the above method using `SemaphoreSlim` to limit the number of concurrent asynchronous operations. The following code snippet demonstrates the more refined approach.

```
/// <summary>
/// Optimized approach with limit concurrency
/// </summary>
/// <returns></returns>
public static async Task OptimizedApproachAsync(List<string> items, int
maxConcurrency = 10)
{
    using (var semaphore = new SemaphoreSlim(maxConcurrency))
    {
        var tasks = items.Select(async item =>
        {
            await semaphore.WaitAsync(); // Limit concurrency by waiting for the
semaphore.
            try
            {
                await ProcessItem(item);
            }
            finally
            {
                semaphore.Release(); // Release the semaphore to allow other
operations.
            }
        });
      await Task.WhenAll(tasks);
    }
}
```

The aforementioned code prevents the system choked by too many concurrent tasks.

Best Practices

Please find below the best practices

Limit Concurrency

To balance system load and resources, it is recommended to use `SemaphoreSlim`

Avoid Blocking Calls

Avoid using `.Result` or `.Wait()` as they can lead to deadlocks and degrade performance.

Async all the way

Avoid mixing async and sync code, ensure all methods are async from top to bottom to prevent deadlock and make optimal use of resources.

Conclusion

Asynchronous programming in C# involves more than just understanding the `async` and `await` keywords; it requires more features like concurrency, resource utilization, and code structure

Day 15 of 30-Day .NET Challenge: Lazy Initialization

To unlock the full potential of your .Net Application, it's essential to familiarize yourself with the Lazy<T> class.

Introduction

To enhance the power of the .Net Application, make use of Lazy<T> class to pause the instantiation of class until the object is needed.

Learning Objectives

- A common mistake of developers
- How to use Lazy<T> class

Prerequisites for Developers

A basic understanding of C# language.

Getting Started

Developers common mistake

Developers often make objects instantiated as soon as the application starts or when a class is instantiated, regardless of whether they are immediately needed or not.

```
// Initializing expensive resources upfront
private readonly ExpensiveObject _expensiveObject = new ExpensiveObject();
public ExpensiveObject ExpensiveObject => _expensiveObject;
```

The _expensiveObject can lead to wasted resources and reduced performance, especially if the ExpensiveObject is not used immediately or ever during the application's lifecycle.

Efficient Method

The syntax for utilizing Lazy<T> is as follows:

```
// Using Lazy<T> to initialize resources only when needed
private readonly Lazy<ExpensiveObject> _expensiveObject = new
Lazy<ExpensiveObject>();
public ExpensiveObject ExpensiveObject => _expensiveObject.Value;
```

The approach shifted to instantiate an object only when it needed. The .Net makes it easier to implement using Lazy<T> syntax and also safe.

Complete Example

First, let's define an ExpensiveResource class that simulates a delay

```
using System;
using System.Threading;

class ExpensiveResource
{
    public ExpensiveResource()
    {
        Console.WriteLine("Initializing expensive resource... This might take a
while.");
        // Simulating expensive initialization with a delay
        Thread.Sleep(2000); // Delay for 2 seconds
        Console.WriteLine("Expensive resource initialized!");
    }
    public void UseResource()
    {
        Console.WriteLine("Using the expensive resource.");
    }
}
```

Now, let's create the main part of the application, where `Lazy<T>` is used to initialize the `ExpensiveResource` lazily.

```
using System;
class Program
{
    private static Lazy<ExpensiveResource> _lazyExpensiveResource = new
Lazy<ExpensiveResource>();
    static void Main(string[] args)
    {
        Console.WriteLine("Application started.");
        Console.WriteLine("Press any key to use the expensive resource...");
        Console.ReadKey();
        // Accessing the Value property of _lazyExpensiveResource for the first
time triggers the initialization.
        _lazyExpensiveResource.Value.UseResource();
        Console.WriteLine("Press any key to exit...");
        Console.ReadKey();
    }
}
```

Benefits of Using `Lazy<T>`

- Improved Performance
- Thread Safety

Day 16 of 30-Day .NET Challenge: In-Memory Caching

Challenges are hard when the database resides in a remote machine or experiencing heavy load. The in-memory caching acts as a better implementation to avoid performance bottlenecks.

Introduction

One of the major issues in an application's performance is the time it takes to respond from external data sources mostly databases. Challenges are hard when the database resides in a remote machine or experiencing heavy load. The in-memory caching acts as a better implementation to avoid performance bottlenecks.

Learning Objectives

- How to use in-memory caching
- Key benefits

Prerequisites for Developers

Basic understanding of C# programming language.

Getting Started

Usually, developers directly fetch information or data directly from the database. It is quite straightforward and simple approach but can lead to performance issues when the database is under a heavy load which impacts application performance and hampers UI experience

```
public Product GetProductById(int id)
{
    // Fetching product data from the database every time
    var product = _dbContext.Products.FirstOrDefault(p => p.Id == id);
    return product;
}
```

How to implement in-memory caching

In-memory caching involves temporarily storing frequently accessed data in the memory of the application server, drastically reducing the need to retrieve data from the database for each request.

```
private static MemoryCache _cache = new MemoryCache(new MemoryCacheOptions());

public Product GetProductById(int id)
{
    // Fetching product data from the cache if available
    if (!_cache.TryGetValue(id, out Product product))
    {
        product = _dbContext.Products.FirstOrDefault(p => p.Id == id);
        _cache.Set(id, product, TimeSpan.FromMinutes(30));
    }
    return product;
}
```

To use MemoryCache, you need to add the Microsoft.Extensions.Caching.Memory package to your project.

```
dotnet add package Microsoft.Extensions.Caching.Memory
```

Create a class InMemoryCache with function named GetProductById which returns a class object of type Product

```
public static class InMemoryCache
{
    private static MemoryCache _cache = new MemoryCache(new MemoryCacheOptions());
    private static ProductRepository _productRepository = new ProductRepository();
    public static Product GetProductById(int id)
    {
        if (!_cache.TryGetValue(id, out Product product))
        {
            Console.WriteLine("Fetching from database...");
            product = _productRepository.GetProductById(id);
            _cache.Set(id, product, TimeSpan.FromMinutes(30)); // Cache for 30
minutes
        }
        else
        {
            Console.WriteLine("Fetching from cache...");
        }
       return product;
    }
}
```

Simulate the ProductRepository and relevant Product class

```
// Simulating a product repository
public class ProductRepository
{
    public Product GetProductById(int id)
    {
        // Simulate database access
        return new Product { Id = id, Name = $"Product {id}" };
    }
}

public class Product
{
    public int Id { get; set; }
    public string Name { get; set; }
}
```

Call from the main method as follows and relevant console output showcasing data fetched from memory.

```
#region Day 16: In-Memory Cache

Console.WriteLine("Fetching product with ID 1 for the first time:");
var product = InMemoryCache.GetProductById(1);
Console.WriteLine($"Product Name: {product.Name}\n");
Console.WriteLine("Fetching product with ID 1 again:");
product = InMemoryCache.GetProductById(1); // This time, it should come from the
cache
Console.WriteLine($"Product Name: {product.Name}\n");
#endregion
```

```
Fetching product with ID 1 for the first time:
Fetching from database...
Product Name: Product 1

Fetching product with ID 1 again:
Fetching from cache...
Product Name: Product 1
```

Key Benefits

- Reduce database load
- Improved application performance
- Scalability

Day 17 of 30-Day .NET Challenge: Interlocked Class

The .Net provide a powerful tool called the "Interlocked" class for all atomic operations through which developers can reduce contention and improve the performance of the application.

Introduction

In multi-threaded application scenarios, using traditional locking techniques can sometimes cause performance bottlenecks for atomic operations. The .Net provide a powerful tool called the "Interlocked" class for all atomic operations through which developers can reduce contention and improve the performance of the application.

Learning Objectives

- Problem with locks
- Using Interlocked classes

Prerequisites for Developers

Basic understanding of C# programming language

Getting Started

Understanding the problem with locks

Traditionally, to ensure thread safety when multiple threads access a shared resource, developers use locks. Locking prevents multiple threads from entering a critical section of code simultaneously, thus ensuring that only one thread at a time can modify the shared resource.

```
private int _counter;
private readonly object _syncRoot = new object();

public void IncrementCounter()
{
    lock (_syncRoot)
    {
        _counter++;
    }
}
```

The aforementioned approach introduces a risk of potential performance issue called contention wherein when multiple threads try to access the lock simultaneously, they are put on hold except for the one that successfully gets the lock.

The Interlocked Class: A Better Way

The .NET framework offers the `Interlocked` class as a part of the `System.Threading` namespace, designed to perform atomic operations efficiently. Atomic operations are indivisible; they complete entirely without interruption.

```
private int _counter;

public void IncrementCounter()
{
    Interlocked.Increment(ref _counter);
}
```

As `Interlocked` class does not require locks so it solves the issue of contention as mentioned in the traditional approach.

Complete Example

Add a new class name `IncrementClass` and add the following code snippet

46/79

```
public static class IncrementClass
{
    private static int _counter = 0;
    /// <summary>
    /// Outputs
    /// Counter value: 10
    /// </summary>
    public static void TestIncrementCounter()
    {
        // Create an array to hold the tasks
        Task[] tasks = new Task[10];
        // Initialize and start tasks
        for (int i = 0; i < tasks.Length; i++)
        {
            tasks[i] = Task.Run(() => IncrementCounter());
        }
        // Wait for all tasks to complete
        Task.WaitAll(tasks);
        Console.WriteLine($"Counter value: {_counter}");
    }
    public static void IncrementCounter()
    {
        // Safely increment the counter across multiple threads
        Interlocked.Increment(ref _counter);
    }
}
```

Call from the main method as follows

```
#region Day 17: Increment Class
IncrementClass.TestIncrementCounter();
#endregion
```

Console output

```
Counter value: 10
```

Day 18 of 30-Day .NET Challenge: AggressiveInlining Attribute

It influences the Just-In-Time (JIT) compiler's behaviour to enhance the execution speed of critical methods.

Introduction

One of the techniques to improve application performance involves the use of the AggressiveInlining attribute. It influences the Just-In-Time (JIT) compiler's behaviour to enhance the execution speed of critical methods.

Learning Objectives

- An example without an AggressiveInlining attribute
- An example with an AgressiveInlining attribute

- When to Use AggressiveInlining

Prerequisites for Developers

Basic understanding of C# programming language.

Getting Started

Example Without AggressiveInlining

Consider a simple method that multiplies its input by two:

```
private int MultiplyByTwo(int value)
{
    return value * 2;
}
```

Without the AggressiveInlining attribute, the JIT compiler may or may not inline this method. The method is not inlined, the overhead of the method calls could impact the application's overall performance.

Example With AggressiveInlining

By marking the method with the AggressiveInlining attribute, it can explicitly signal the JIT compiler:

```
using System.Runtime.CompilerServices;

[MethodImpl(MethodImplOptions.AggressiveInlining)]
private int MultiplyByTwo(int value)
{
    return value * 2;
}
```

In this scenario, the JIT compiler is going to inline the method, reducing the overhead and improving the performance of code that frequently calls this method.

When to Use AggressiveInlining.

While AggressiveInlining can be a powerful tool for optimizing methods, it should be used carefully.

Overuse or inappropriate use of the attribute can lead to larger code size (code bloat), which might negatively impact performance by affecting cache utilization.

It's best to reserve AggressiveInlining for small, critical methods where the benefits of inlining outweigh the potential drawbacks.

Complete Code

Add a class named "AggressiveInlining" with two methods as shown below highlighting the difference between a method with AggressiveInlining and one with not.

```
public static class AggressiveInlining
{
    public static int MultiplyByTwo(int value)
    {
        return value * 2;
    }
    [MethodImpl(MethodImplOptions.AggressiveInlining)]
    public static int MultiplyByTwoWithAggressiveInlining(int value)
    {
        return value * 2;
    }
}
```

Call from the main method as follows

```
#region Day 18: AggressiveInlining Attribute
AggressiveInlining.MultiplyByTwo(10);
AggressiveInlining.MultiplyByTwoWithAggressiveInlining(10);
#endregion
```

Day 19 of 30-Day .NET Challenge: Stack vs. Heap Allocation

The article demonstrates the idea of memory allocations to be used for vibrant and high-performance applications.

Introduction

The article demonstrates the idea of memory allocations to be used for vibrant and high-performance applications. There are majorly two types of memory allocation i.e. stack vs heap which plays a role in how your application uses resources and, further, how fast and responsive the application can be.

Learning Objectives

- What is heap allocation
- What is stack allocation
- Limiting the Use of Heap-Allocated Objects

Prerequisites for Developers

Basic understanding of C# programming language.

Getting Started

What is heap allocation?

The heap memory is primarily used for dynamic allocation, where the size and lifespan of the allocation are not predicted at the compile time. Reference types instances (like objects and arrays in C#) are stored on the heap.

What is stack allocation?

The stack is a section of memory that stores value types and pointers to heap-allocated objects. Memory allocation on the stack is fast because it involves merely moving the stack pointer.

Limiting the Use of Heap-Allocated Objects

Whenever possible, opt for stack allocation or the use of value types to minimize the need for garbage collection.

Inefficient Heap Allocation

The following method creates a new string object on the heap each time the method is called, which will call the Garbage Collection each time too.

```
private string GetUserName(int index)
{
    // Inefficient: Creates a new string object on the heap
    return new string($"User{index}".ToCharArray());
}
```

Efficient Allocation

By returning the interpolated string without new keyword avoids unnecessary heap allocation and reduces the impact on garbage collection, which leads to better performance.

```
private string GetUserName(int index)
{
    // Efficient: Avoids unnecessary heap allocation
    return $"User{index}";
}
```

Create another class named `StackVsHeap` and add the following code snippet

```
public static class StackVsHeap
{
    public static string InefficientMethod(int index)
    {
        // Inefficient: Creates a new string object on the heap
        return new string($"User{index}".ToCharArray());
    }

    public static string EfficientMethod(int index)
    {
        // Efficient: Avoids unnecessary heap allocation
        return $"User{index}";
    }
}
```

Execute from the main method as follows

```
#region Day 19: Stack vs. Heap Allocation
static string ExecuteDay19()
{
    StackVsHeap.InefficientMethod(0);
    StackVsHeap.EfficientMethod(0);
    return "Executed Day 19 successfully..!!";
}

#endregion
```

Console output

```
User0
User0
```

Day 20 of 30-Day .NET Challenge: Task vs. ValueTask

Heap allocations aren't entirely bad but when an object is allocated on a heap it contributes to the garbage collection cycles which in turn reduces overall application performance.

Introduction

One approach to optimize resource usage in async code is by using `ValueTask<TResult>` syntax to minimize heap allocations, which in turn reduces pressure on garbage collection and enhances overall performance.

Learning Objectives

- The Problem with Heap Allocations
- Optimizing with `ValueTask<TResult>`
- When to Use `ValueTask<TResult>`

Prerequisites for Developers

Basic understanding of C# programming language.

Getting Started

Heap allocations aren't entirely bad but when an object is allocated on a heap it contributes to the garbage collection cycles which in turn reduces overall application performance. In case of excessive heap allocation, the garbage collector can lead to GC pauses.

Bad Practice: Excessive Use of Task<TResult>

Let's consider a common asynchronous pattern that developers commonly use:

```
public async Task<string> ReadDataAsync()
{
    var data = await ReadFromStreamAsync(_stream);
    return ProcessData(data);
}
```

If the above-mentioned method is called more frequently, each request results in a new Task instance being allocated on heap memory. Over time, it leads to increased garbage collection overhead.

Optimizing with ValueTask<TResult>

By changing the return type from `Task<TResult>` to `ValueTask<TResult>`, we can reduce heap allocations

```
public async ValueTask<string> ReadDataAsync()
{
    var data = await ReadFromStreamAsync(_stream);
    return ProcessData(data);
}
```

The aforementioned optimization is beneficial for high-frequency async operations or methods which are expected to complete synchronously in a significant portion of time.

When to Use ValueTask<TResult>

- High-frequency methods
- Performance-sensitive code
- Methods that often complete synchronously

Create another class named `TaskVsValueTask` and add the following code snippet

```
public static class TaskVsValueTask
{
    public static async Task<string> FetchDataAsync()
    {
        // Simulate a delay to mimic fetching data
        await Task.Delay(1000);
        return "Data fetched using Task";
    }

    public static async ValueTask<string> FetchDataValueTaskAsync()
    {
        // Simulate a delay to mimic fetching data
        await Task.Delay(1000); // Note: Use Task.Delay for the sake of example.
        return "Data fetched using ValueTask";
    }
}
```

Execute from the main method as follows

52/79

```
#region Day 20: Task vs. Value Task
static async Task<string> ExecuteDay20()
{
    Console.WriteLine("Fetching data with Task...");
    string result = await TaskVsValueTask.FetchDataAsync();
    Console.WriteLine(result);
    Console.WriteLine("Fetching data with ValueTask...");
    string resultValueTask = await TaskVsValueTask.FetchDataValueTaskAsync();
    Console.WriteLine(resultValueTask);
    return "Executed Day 20 successfully..!!";
}
#endregion
```

Console Output

```
Fetching data with Task...
Data fetched using Task
Fetching data with ValueTask...
Data fetched using ValueTask
```

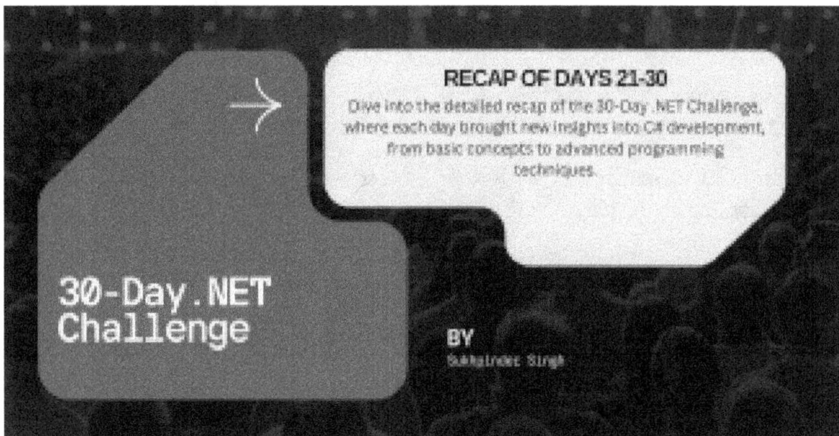
RECAP OF DAYS 21-30
Dive into the detailed recap of the 30-Day .NET Challenge, where each day brought new insights into C# development, from basic concepts to advanced programming techniques.
30-Day.NET Challenge
BY

Day 21 of 30-Day .NET Challenge: StringComparison

The article demonstrates the importance of using `StringComparison` options for efficient string comparison in .NET

Introduction

Whether it's searching, sorting or equality; how you compare strings can significantly impact your application performance. The article demonstrates the importance of using `StringComparison` options for efficient string comparison in .NET

Learning Objectives

- The Problem with Inefficient String Comparisons

- Efficient String Comparison with StringComparison
- Choosing the Right StringComparison Option

Prerequisites for Developers

Basic understanding of C# programming language.

Getting Started

The Problem with Inefficient String Comparisons

Consider the following common approach used by most developers for string comparison:

```
// Inefficient string comparison
bool equal = string1.ToLower() == string2.ToLower();
```

- The `ToLower` method creates a new string memory allocation for each comparison, leading to unnecessary allocations. Consider a method with frequent requests that can degrade the application performance.
- The `ToLower` method is culture-sensitive, which means it might produce different results depending on the current culture set in the executing thre

.NET provides a powerful enumeration, `StringComparison`, designed to address these inefficiencies.

```
// Efficient string comparison
bool equal = string.Equals(string1, string2, StringComparison.OrdinalIgnoreCase);
```

- **Ordinal:** Use for most general-purpose comparisons where cultural rules are not relevant. This is the fastest option.
- **OrdinalIgnoreCase:** Ideal for case-insensitive comparisons where cultural rules do not apply.
- **CurrentCulture and CurrentCultureIgnoreCase:** Use when comparing strings displayed to the user, where adherence to cultural rules is important.
- **InvariantCulture and InvariantCultureIgnoreCase:** Suitable for scenarios requiring consistency across different cultures, such as storing and retrieving data.

Create another class named `StringComparisons` and add the following code snippet

```
public static class StringComparisons
{
    private static readonly string string1 = "test";
    private static readonly string string2 = "test";
    public static void BadMethod()
    {
        // Inefficient string comparison
        bool equal = string1.ToLower() == string2.ToLower();
        Console.WriteLine($"In bad method strings are {equal}");
    }
    public static void GoodMethod()
    {
        // efficient string comparison
        bool equal = string.Equals(string1, string2,
System.StringComparison.OrdinalIgnoreCase);
        Console.WriteLine($"In good method strings are {equal}");
    }
}
```

Execute from the main method as follows

```
#region Day 21: String Comparisons
static string ExecuteDay21()
{
    StringComparisons.BadMethod();
    StringComparisons.GoodMethod();
    return "Executed Day 21 successfully..!!";
}
#endregion
```

Console output

```
In bad method strings are True
In good method strings are True
```

Introduction

Frequent allocation and deallocation of bigger buffers can impact performance due to the increased work on the garbage collector. The recommendation is to us `ArrayPool<T>`, a mechanism to recycle temporary buffers and optimize performance by reducing garbage collection cycles.

Learning Objectives

- Understanding the Problem with Traditional Buffer Allocation
- The Approach Using `ArrayPool<T>`
- Best Practices for Using `ArrayPool<T>`

Getting Started

A common approach developers use involves directly allocating a new buffer

```
// Allocating a new large buffer
byte[] buffer = new byte[4096];
```

While the aforementioned code snippet looks clean and straightforward, it has significant drawbacks regarding performance, particularly in applications that frequently request large temporary buffers. Each allocation will increase the heap size, leading to more frequent garbage collection.

`ArrayPool<T>` is part of the `System.Buffers` namespace and provides temporary arrays, thereby reducing the need for frequent memory allocations and GC.

```
// Using ArrayPool<T> to recycle large buffers
var pool = ArrayPool<byte>.Shared;
byte[] buffer = pool.Rent(4096);
try
{
    // Work with the buffer
}
finally
{
    pool.Return(buffer);
}
```

Best Practices for Using ArrayPool<T>

While `ArrayPool<T>` can significantly enhance performance, there are best practices to ensure its effective use:

- **Properly Return Buffers**: Always return the rented buffers to the pool in a `finally` block to ensure that they are returned even if an exception occurs.
- **Clear Buffers When Necessary**: If sensitive data is stored in the buffer, use the overload of the `Return` method that takes a boolean parameter indicating whether the buffer should be cleared.
- **Avoid Holding Buffers for Long Periods**: Rent buffers for the shortest time necessary to keep the pool efficient and avoid exhausting the pool.

Complete Code

Create another class named `ArrayPoolExample` and add the following code snippet

```
public static class ArrayPoolExample
{
    public static void BadMethod()
    {
        // Allocating a new large buffer
        byte[] buffer = new byte[4096];
        // Simulate work with the buffer
        FillBuffer(buffer, 0xAA); // Example operation
        Console.WriteLine("Buffer used and will be discarded after method
execution.");
    }
    public static void GoodMethod()
    {
        var pool = ArrayPool<byte>.Shared;
        byte[] buffer = pool.Rent(4096);
        try
        {
            // Work with the buffer
            FillBuffer(buffer, 0xBB); // Example operation
            Console.WriteLine("Buffer rented from the pool and returned after
use.");
        }
        finally
        {
            pool.Return(buffer);
        }
    }
    public static void FillBuffer(byte[] buffer, byte value)
    {
        for (int i = 0; i < buffer.Length; i++)
        {
            buffer[i] = value;
        }
        // Just an example to simulate buffer usage
        Console.WriteLine($"Buffer filled with value: {value}");
    }
}
```

Execute from the main method as follows

```
#region Day 22: Array Pool
static string ExecuteDay22()
{
  Console.WriteLine("Demonstrating BAD Method:");
    ArrayPoolExample.BadMethod();
    Console.WriteLine("\nDemonstrating GOOD Method:");
    ArrayPoolExample.GoodMethod();
    return "Executed Day 22 successfully..!!";
}
#endregion
```

Console Output

```
Demonstrating BAD Method:
Buffer filled with value: 170
Buffer used and will be discarded after method execution.

Demonstrating GOOD Method:
Buffer filled with value: 187
Buffer rented from the pool and returned after use.
```

Optimization involves choosing Span<T> over Arrays for manipulating memory regions. Discover a better approach using Spans on Day 23 of our 30-Day .NET Challenge.

Introduction

The article demonstrates the use of Span<T> for optimizing memory management, highlighting the performance benefits.

Learning Objectives

- Drawbacks of the array in memory management
- Efficiency of Spans

Prerequisites for Developers

Basic understanding of C# programming language.

Generally, developers use an array to store sequences of elements in continuous memory locations. Arrays are quite simple and easy to understand. A code snippet of the byte array is shown below

```
// Bad way: Using arrays may lead to unnecessary memory allocations and copying
byte[] data = GetData();
ProcessData(data);
```

The problem with the above code is that it may lead to unnecessary memory allocations and copying because GetData creates a new array each time. The aforementioned code block will degrade the performance of the applications that require high data processing or applications that have limited memory resources.

Efficiency of Spans

Please find below the refactored version of the previous code snippet.

```
// Good way: Using Span<T> avoids additional memory allocation and copying
byte[] data = GetData();
Span<byte> dataSpan = data.AsSpan();
ProcessData(dataSpan);
```

The Span<T> provides a type-safe and memory-safe view of contiguous memory regions without worrying about the copy issue highlighted previously.

Using the AsSpan() method creates a view of the original array without copying or creating a new memory each time.

Complete Code

Create another class named SpanOverArray and add the following code snippet

```
public static class SpanOverArray
{
    public static void ProcessData(byte[] data)
    {
        Console.WriteLine("Processing byte array:");
        foreach (var b in data)
        {
            Console.Write($"{b} ");
        }
        Console.WriteLine("\n");
    }
    public static void ProcessData(Span<byte> dataSpan)
    {
        Console.WriteLine("Processing Span<byte>:");
        foreach (var b in dataSpan)
        {
            Console.Write($"{b} ");
        }
        Console.WriteLine("\n");
    }
}
```

Execute from the main method as follows

```
#region Day 23: Span Over Arrays
static string ExecuteDay23()
{
  byte[] largeData = new byte[100]; // Simulate a large data set
    Random rng = new Random();
    rng.NextBytes(largeData); // Populate with random bytes
    // Process using array slice
    byte[] slice = new byte[10]; // Creating a new array for the slice
    Array.Copy(largeData, 10, slice, 0, 10); // Copying data
    SpanOverArray.ProcessData(slice);
    // Process using Span<T>
    Span<byte> span = largeData.AsSpan(10, 10); // Creating a span starting at
index 10
    SpanOverArray.ProcessData(span);
    return "Executed Day 23 successfully..!!";
}
#endregion
```

Console Output

```
Processing byte array:
75 20 132 37 218 170 182 227 224 146
```

```
Processing Span<byte>:
75 20 132 37 218 170 182 227 224 146
```

Day 24 of 30-Day .NET Challenge: Avoid Exceptions in Flow Control

Learn to enhance your C# code's performance and readability by avoiding exceptions for flow control. Discover a better approach using TryParse on Day 24 of our 30-Day .NET Challenge.

Introduction

Exceptions are designed to handle unexpected situations rather than controlling the application flow. Using exceptions during input validation can affect your application's readability and performance.

Learning Objectives

- The inefficient use of exceptions
- A better approach using TryParse

Getting Started

Using exceptions for flow control, especially in a loop or frequently called code, may lead to severe performance bottlenecks. It also makes code hard to understand.

Exceptions are really expensive in terms of system resources because when an exception is triggered, .Net runtime captures the stack trace and the process is resource-intensive.

```
try
{
    int.Parse(input); // Attempt to parse input
}
catch (FormatException)
{
    // Handle the invalid input
}
```

A better approach using TryParse

Please find below the refactored version of the previous code snippet

```
if (int.TryParse(input, out int result))
{
    // Use the parsed value
}
else
{
    // Handle the invalid input
}
```

The aforementioned code attempts to parse the input supplied from the console and returns a boolean whether it's a success or failure.

Complete Code

Create another class named AvoidExceptions and add the following code snippet

```
public static class AvoidExceptions
{
    public static void BadWay(string input)
    {
        // Inefficient way: Using exceptions for flow control
        try
        {
            int number = int.Parse(input);
            Console.WriteLine($"You entered (Exception method): {number}");
        }
        catch (FormatException)
        {
            Console.WriteLine("Invalid input! Please enter a valid integer.");
        }
    }
    public static void GoodWay(string input)
    {
        // Efficient way: Using TryParse for flow control
        if (int.TryParse(input, out int result))
        {
            Console.WriteLine($"You entered (TryParse method): {result}");
        }
        else
        {
            Console.WriteLine("Invalid input! Please enter a valid integer.");
        }
    }
}
```

Execute from the main method as follows

```
#region Day 24: Avoid Exceptions in Flow Control
static string ExecuteDay24()
{
    Console.WriteLine("Enter a number:");
    string input = Console.ReadLine();
    AvoidExceptions.BadWay(input);
    AvoidExceptions.GoodWay(input);
    return "Executed Day 24 successfully..!!";
}
#endregion
```

Console Output

```
Invalid input! Please enter a valid integer.
Invalid input! Please enter a valid integer.
```

Day 25 of 30-Day .NET Challenge: Use Exception Filters

Learn to enhance your C# code's readability by avoiding multiple catch blocks. Discover a better approach using Exception Filters on Day 25 of our 30-Day .NET Challenge.

Introduction

The article demonstrates the use of exception filters to improve the readability, maintainability and performance of the application.

Learning Objectives

- The problem with traditional exception handling.
- Efficient exception handling using filters.

Prerequisites for Developers

Basic understanding of C# programming language.

Getting Started

The problem with traditional exception handling

Tritionally, developers often use simple catch blocks to handle exceptions and use conditional logic to handle specific exception types. Please find below the code snippet demonstrating the traditional approach

```
try
{
    // Perform an operation
}
catch (Exception ex)
{
    if (ex is InvalidOperationException || ex is ArgumentNullException)
    {
        // Handle the specific exceptions
    }
    else
    {
        throw;  // Rethrow the exception if it's not one we're specifically
handling
    }
}
```

Using conditional statements with an if block creates a code which is hard to maintain and doesn't look very reable.

```
try
{
    // Perform an operation
}
catch (Exception ex) when (ex is InvalidOperationException || ex is
ArgumentNullException)
{
    // Handle only InvalidOperationException or ArgumentNullException
}
```

The approach above improves the readability and maintainability of the code. In addition to that, it enhances the performance as the catch block is executed only when the filter evaluates to be true as catching an exception is an expensive operation. Only when the filter returns a true, the stack trace will be captured.

Complete Code

Create another class named `ExceptionFilters` and add the following code snippet

```
public static class ExceptionFilters
{
    public static void MultipleCatch(string input)
    {
        try
        {
            ProcessInput(input);
        }
        catch (Exception ex)
        {
            if (ex is InvalidOperationException || ex is ArgumentNullException)
            {
                Console.WriteLine($"Conventional Handling: Caught
{ex.GetType().Name}");
            }
            else
            {
                throw;
            }
        }
    }
    public static void GoodWay(string input)
    {
        // Using exception filters
        try
        {
            ProcessInput(input);
        }
        catch (Exception ex) when (ex is InvalidOperationException || ex is
ArgumentNullException)
        {
            Console.WriteLine($"Exception Filters Handling: Caught
{ex.GetType().Name}");
        }
    }
    public static void ProcessInput(string input)
    {
        if (input == null)
            throw new ArgumentNullException(nameof(input), "Input cannot be
null.");
        else if (input == "invalid")
            throw new InvalidOperationException("Invalid input provided.");
        Console.WriteLine($"Processing {input}");
    }
}
```

Execute from the main method as follows

```
#region Day 25: Use Exception Filters
static string ExecuteDay25()
{
    // Using conventional exception handling
    // This will cause ArgumentNullException
    ExceptionFilters.MultipleCatch(null);
    // Reset input for valid processing
    ExceptionFilters.GoodWay("Valid input");

    // This input will cause InvalidOperationException
    ExceptionFilters.GoodWay("invalid");
    return "Executed Day 25 successfully..!!";
}
#endregion
```

Console Output

```
Conventional Handling: Caught ArgumentNullException
Processing Valid input
Exception Filters Handling: Caught InvalidOperationException
```

Day 26 of 30-Day .NET Challenge: Loop Unrolling

Learn to enhance your loop performance in C#. Discover a better approach using Loop Unrolling on Day 26 of our 30-Day .NET Challenge.

Introduction

The article demonstrates the advantages of loop unrolling by iterating over multiple items per cycle while adjusting the loop counter accordingly.

Learning Objectives

- The problem with iterating using traditional loops
- Advantages with loop unrolling

Getting Started

The problem with iterating using traditional loops

```
for (int i = 0; i < array.Length; i++)
{
    array[i] = i * 2;
}
```

Although the above code snippet is quite clean and straightforward, it incurs a cost due to the loop control structure.

Advantages with loop unrolling

Please find below the refactored version of the previous code snippet

```
int len = array.Length;
for (int i = 0; i < len; i += 4)
{
    array[i] = i * 2;
    if (i + 1 < len) array[i + 1] = (i + 1) * 2;
    if (i + 2 < len) array[i + 2] = (i + 2) * 2;
    if (i + 3 < len) array[i + 3] = (i + 3) * 2;
}
```

In addition to that, it will reduce

- Reduce loop overheads which in turn decreases any conditional checks inside the loops.
- Increase performance as it enhances the execution speed

Complete Code

Create another class named LoopUnrolling and add the following code snippet

```
public static class LoopUnrolling
{
    public static void BadWay() {
        const int size = 1024;
        int[] numbers = new int[size];
    // Traditional loop
        var watch = System.Diagnostics.Stopwatch.StartNew();
        for (int i = 0; i < numbers.Length; i++)
        {
            numbers[i] = i * 2;
        }
        watch.Stop();
        Console.WriteLine($"Traditional loop time: {watch.ElapsedTicks} ticks");
    }
    public static void GoodWay()
    {
        const int size = 1024;
        int[] numbers = new int[size];
        int len = numbers.Length;
        var watch = System.Diagnostics.Stopwatch.StartNew();
        for (int i = 0; i < len; i += 4)
        {
            numbers[i] = i * 2;
            if (i + 1 < len) numbers[i + 1] = (i + 1) * 2;
            if (i + 2 < len) numbers[i + 2] = (i + 2) * 2;
            if (i + 3 < len) numbers[i + 3] = (i + 3) * 2;
        }
        watch.Stop();
        Console.WriteLine($"Unrolled loop time: {watch.ElapsedTicks} ticks");
    }
}
```

Execute from the main method as follows

```
#region Day 26: Loop Unrolling
static string ExecuteDay26()
{
    LoopUnrolling.BadWay();
    LoopUnrolling.GoodWay();
    return "Executed Day 26 successfully..!!";
}
#endregion
```

Console Output

```
Traditional loop time: 20 ticks
Unrolled loop time: 12 ticks
```

As the output demonstrates loop unrolling took much less time than the traditional loop approach.

Day 27 of 30-Day .NET Challenge: Query v/s Method Syntax

Learn why query syntax is preferred in LINQ. Discover a better approach using Query Syntax on Day 27 of our 30-Day .NET Challenge.

Introduction

The article demonstrates the use of query and method syntax for writing LINQ queries. In addition to that, highlights why the query syntax is preferred over method syntax in case of complex queries.

Learning Objectives

- Why Query Syntax is preferred

Getting Started

Before diving in let's understand each syntax for LINQ.

Method Syntax

```
var query = items.Where(item => item.IsActive)
                 .Select(item => new { item.Name, item.Id });
```

As the queries become more complex in nature, the syntax is not readable.

```
var query = from item in items
            where item.IsActive
            select new { item.Name, item.Id };
```

The aforementioned syntax is quite similar to SQL query structure, which makes it more understandable, readable and maintainable.

Consider an example wherein we need to join two collections, filter them and map them into a new type. Let's solve the above problem statement using both of the syntaxes.

Method Syntax

The following implementation seems more dense and complex.

```
var query = items.Join(otherCollection,
                       item => item.Key,
                       other => other.Key,
                       (item, other) => new { item.Name, other.Description })
                .Where(x => x.Description.Contains("specific keyword"))
                .Select(x => new { x.Name, x.Description });
```

Query Syntax

Rewriting the same query using query syntax makes it more readable and understandable.

```
var query = from item in items
            join other in otherCollection on item.Key equals other.Key
            where other.Description.Contains("specific keyword")
            select new { item.Name, other.Description };
```

Complete Code

Create another class named QueryVsMethod and add the following code snippet

```
public static class QueryVsMethod
{
    static List<Item> items = new List<Item>
    {
        new Item { Id = 1, Name = "Item1", IsActive = true },
        new Item { Id = 2, Name = "Item2", IsActive = false },
        new Item { Id = 3, Name = "Item3", IsActive = true }
    };
    public static void QuerySyntax()
    {
        // Method Syntax
        var methodSyntaxQuery = items.Where(item => item.IsActive)
                                     .Select(item => new { item.Name, item.Id });
        Console.WriteLine("Method Syntax Results:");
        foreach (var item in methodSyntaxQuery)
        {
            Console.WriteLine($"Name: {item.Name}, Id: {item.Id}");
        }
    }
    public static void MethodSyntax()
    {
        // Query Syntax
        var querySyntaxQuery = from item in items
                               where item.IsActive
                               select new { item.Name, item.Id };
        Console.WriteLine("\nQuery Syntax Results:");
        foreach (var item in querySyntaxQuery)
        {
            Console.WriteLine($"Name: {item.Name}, Id: {item.Id}");
        }
    }
}

class Item
{
    public int Id { get; set; }
    public string Name { get; set; }
    public bool IsActive { get; set; }
}

#region Day 27: Query vs Method Syntax
static string ExecuteDay27()
{
    QueryVsMethod.MethodSyntax();
    QueryVsMethod.QuerySyntax();
    return "Executed Day 27 successfully..!!";
}
#endregion
```

Console Output

```
Query Syntax Results:
Name: Item1, Id: 1
Name: Item3, Id: 3
Method Syntax Results:
Name: Item1, Id: 1
Name: Item3, Id: 3
```

Day 28 of 30-Day .NET Challenge: Use Stackalloc

Introduction

.Net applications rely on a Garbage collector for memory allocation and deallocation, which simplifies memory management but leads to performance degradation if not managed efficiently. The article demonstrates how to use stackalloc to enhance application performance.

Learning Objectives

- Understanding what is stackalloc
- Problem with traditional heap allocation
- Basic understanding of C# programming language.
- Familiar with for loops

Getting Started

Stackalloc is a reserved keyword in C# which helps to allocate memory on the stack instead of heap which is managed by Garbage Collector whereas stack allocation is automatically freed once method execution ends.

Problem with traditional heap allocation

Consider the following code example wherein the memory for the `double array` is allocation on the heap.

```
private double CalculateSum(double[] values)
{
    double sum = 0;
    for (int i = 0; i < values.Length; i++)
    {
        sum += values[i];
    }
    return sum;
}
```

Optimal use of stackalloc

Please find below the refactored version of the previous code snippet

```
private unsafe double CalculateSum(int count)
{
    double sum = 0;
    double* values = stackalloc double[count];  // Allocate memory on the stack
    for (int i = 0; i < count; i++)
    {
        values[i] = SomeValue(i);  // Assume SomeValue is a method returning a
double
        sum += values[i];
    }
    return sum;
}
```

In the above method, the values are allocated on stack rather than heap. In this approach there is no need for garbage collection, leading to faster execution and can reduce the pressure on GC.

For performance-sensitive applications, memory management is critical hence using stackalloc a developer can perform memory allocation/deallocation efficiently.

Complete Code

```
public static class StackAlloc
{
    static int count = 10000;  // Number of elements
    static double[] values = new double[count];
    public static void BadWay() {
      FillValues(values);
        // Calculate sum using heap allocation
        double heapSum = CalculateSumHeap(values);
        Console.WriteLine($"Heap allocation sum: {heapSum}");
    }
    public static void GoodWay()
    {
        FillValues(values);
        // Calculate sum using stackalloc
        double stackSum = CalculateSumStackalloc(count);
        Console.WriteLine($"Stackalloc sum: {stackSum}");
    }
    private static void FillValues(double[] values)
    {
        for (int i = 0; i < values.Length; i++)
        {
            values[i] = SomeValue(i);
        }
    }
    private static double SomeValue(int i)
    {
        // Just a sample value function
        return i * 2.5;
    }
    private static double CalculateSumHeap(double[] values)
    {
        double sum = 0;
        for (int i = 0; i < values.Length; i++)
        {
            sum += values[i];
        }
        return sum;
    }
    private static unsafe double CalculateSumStackalloc(int count)
    {
        double sum = 0;
        double* values = stackalloc double[count];
        for (int i = 0; i < count; i++)
        {
            values[i] = SomeValue(i);
            sum += values[i];
        }
        return sum;
    }
}
```

Execute from the main method as follows

```
#region Day 28: Use Stackalloc
static string ExecuteDay28()
{
    StackAlloc.BadWay();
    StackAlloc.GoodWay();

    return "Executed Day 28 successfully..!!";
}
#endregion
```

Console Output

```
Heap allocation sum: 124987500
Stackalloc sum: 124987500
```

Day 29 of 30-Day .NET Challenge: Generics & Custom Interfaces

Learn to enhance your maintainability with generics and custom interfaces in C#. Discover a better approach on Day 29 of our 30-Day .NET Challenge.

Introduction

Developers often tend to add unnecessary boxing in the code which can hamper application performance. The article demonstrates both inefficient and efficient approaches to avoid the issue.

Learning Objectives

- What is Boxing
- Why non-generic interface approach is inefficient
- A recommended approach using generics

Getting Started

Boxing is the process of converting a value type into an object type. In other words, it means the allocation of objects on a heap rather than a stack. Therefore, a performance overhead because of increased memory usage and the need for garbage collection.

In the following scenario, each time a value is assigned to values, it undergoes boxing which can make your application suffer from performance pressure.

```
public interface INumber
{
    object Value { get; set; }
}

public class Number : INumber
{
    public object Value { get; set; }
}
```

Please find below the refactored version of the previous code snippet using generics which allows type safety without the need for boxing.

```
public interface INumber<T>
{
    T Value { get; set; }
}

public class Number<T> : INumber<T> // Utilize generics to avoid boxing
{
    public T Value { get; set; }
}
```

How to use Generics in practice

```
var intNumber = new Number<int> { Value = 123 };
var floatNumber = new Number<float> { Value = 123.45f };
```

Complete Code

Create another class named `GenericCustomInterfaces` and add the following code snippet

```
public static class GenericCustomInterfaces
{
  static List<INumber<int>> intNumbers = new List<INumber<int>>();
  static List<INumber<double>> doubleNumbers = new List<INumber<double>>();
  public static void Example()
  {
      // Populate the list with integers
      for (int i = 0; i < 10; i++)
      {
          intNumbers.Add(new Number<int>(i));
      }
      // Populate the list with doubles
      for (double d = 0.5; d < 10.0; d += 1.0)
      {
          doubleNumbers.Add(new Number<double>(d));
      }
      // Process and display integer numbers
      Console.WriteLine("Integer Numbers:");
      foreach (var num in intNumbers)
      {
          Console.WriteLine(num.Value);
      }
      // Process and display double numbers
      Console.WriteLine("\nDouble Numbers:");
      foreach (var num in doubleNumbers)
      {
          Console.WriteLine(num.Value);
      }
  }
}
```

Add the interface and its class implementation as follows

```
public interface INumber<T>
{
    T Value { get; set; }
}
public class Number<T> : INumber<T>
{
    public T Value { get; set; }
    public Number(T value)
    {
        Value = value;
    }
}
```

Execute from the main method as follows

```
#region Day 29: Generics & Custom Interfaces
static string ExecuteDay29()
{
    GenericCustomInterfaces.Example();
    return "Executed Day 29 successfully..!!";
}
#endregion
```

Console Output

```
Integer Numbers:
0
1
2
3
4
5
6
7
8
9

Double Numbers:
0.5
1.5
2.5
3.5
4.5
5.5
6.5
7.5
8.5
9.5
```

Day 30 of 30-Day .NET Challenge: XML v/s JSON Serialization

Learn to enhance your code with JSON Serialization in C#. Discover a better approach on Day 30 of our 30-Day .NET Challenge.

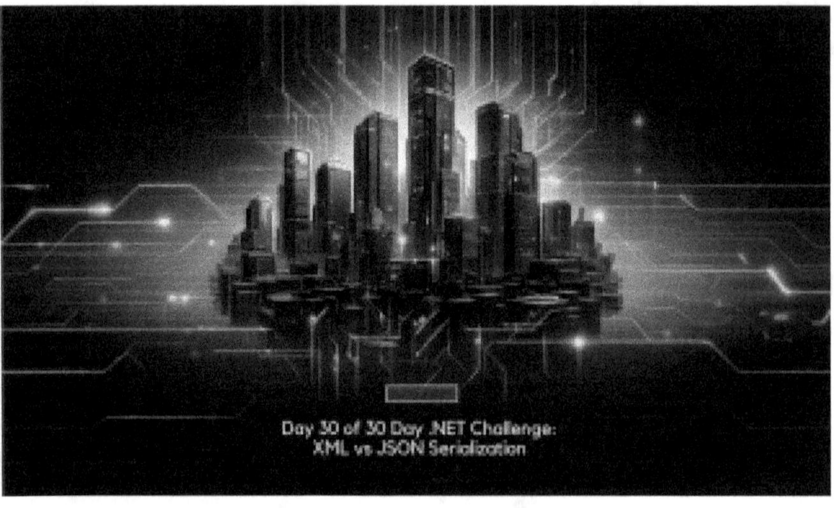
Day 30 of 30 Day .NET Challenge:
XML vs JSON Serialization

Introduction

Serialization involves a process of converting an object into an easily stored format. The article demonstrates the problem with old XML Serialization and how JSON serialization improves both efficiency and effectiveness.

Learning Objectives

- Drawbacks of XML Serialization
- Advantages of JSON Serialization

Prerequisites for Developers

Basic understanding of C# programming language.

Getting Started

Drawbacks of XML Serialization

Traditionally many developers have used XML Serialization as demonstrated in the following code snippet.

```
// Using XmlSerializer for data serialization
private string SerializeObjectToXml<T>(T obj)
{
    var serializer = new XmlSerializer(typeof(T));
    using (var writer = new StringWriter())
    {
        serializer.Serialize(writer, obj);
        return writer.ToString();
    }
}
```

Even though XML is human-readable and globally supported it is not an optimized and efficient choice of serialization in the C# programming language. The main reason is that it involves a lot of temporary objects which can impact the memory usage and the corresponding GC pressure.

Advantages of JSON Serialization

Please find below the refactored version of the previous code snippet using `NewtonSoft.Json` library

```
// Using Newtonsoft.Json for data serialization
private string SerializeObjectToJson<T>(T obj)
{
    return JsonConvert.SerializeObject(obj);
}
```

The aforementioned library outperforms `XmlSerializer` in both speed and efficiency. In addition to that, the JSON files are smaller in size which makes reading and writing faster.

Complete Code

Create another class named `EfficientSerialization` and add the following code snippet

```
public static class EfficientSerialization
{
    public static string XML<T>(T obj)
    {
      var serializer = new XmlSerializer(typeof(T));
        using (var writer = new StringWriter())
        {
            serializer.Serialize(writer, obj);
            return writer.ToString();
        }
    }
    public static string JSON<T>(T obj)
    {
        return JsonConvert.SerializeObject(obj);
    }
}
```

And create a model class as follows

```
public class Person
{
    public string Name { get; set; }
    public int Age { get; set; }
}
```

Execute from the main method as follows

```
#region Day 30: Efficient Serialization
static string ExecuteDay30()
{
    Person person = new Person { Name = "John Doe", Age = 30 };
    // XML Serialization
    string xmlData = EfficientSerialization.XML(person);
    Console.WriteLine("XML Serialization Output:");
    Console.WriteLine(xmlData);
    // JSON Serialization
    string jsonData = EfficientSerialization.JSON(person);
    Console.WriteLine("JSON Serialization Output:");
    Console.WriteLine(jsonData);
    return "Executed Day 30 successfully..!!";
}
#endregion
```

Console Output

```
XML Serialization Output:
<?xml version="1.0" encoding="utf-16"?>
<Person xmlns:xsi="http://www.w3.org/2001/XMLSchema-instance"
xmlns:xsd="http://www.w3.org/2001/XMLSchema">
  <Name>John Doe</Name>
  <Age>30</Age>
</Person>

JSON Serialization Output:
{"Name":"John Doe","Age":30}
```

www.ingramcontent.com/pod-product-compliance
Lightning Source LLC
LaVergne TN
LVHW051605050326
832903LV00033B/4373

* 9 7 9 8 3 3 4 7 2 6 9 6 3 *